2021 SHAMAN MOON DIARY

2021

Shaman Moon Diary

https://www.facebook.com/Psychicx

Published by Mystic Cat Press

Suite SM-2380-6403

14601 North Bybee Lake Court

Portland, Oregon 97203

Phone: +1 (805) 308-6503

Crystal@psychic-emails.com

Copyright © 2020 by Mystic Cat Press

All rights reserved. This book or any portion thereof may not be reproduced or used in any manner whatsoever without the publisher's express written permission except for the use of brief quotations in a book review.

The information accessible from this book is for informational purposes only. None of the information within should be regarded as a promise of benefits, a warranty, or a guarantee of results to be achieved.

Images are used under license from Shutterstock, Dreamstime, or Deposit-photos.

Shaman Moon Diary

2021

The Moon Phases

- New Moon (Dark Moon)
- Waxing Crescent Moon
- First Quarter Moon
- Waxing Gibbous Moon
- Full Moon
- Waning Gibbous (Disseminating) Moon
- Third (Last/Reconciling) Quarter Moon
- Waning Crescent (Balsamic) Moon

🌑 New Moon (Dark Moon)

The New Moon is all about discovering what hides beyond the realm of everyday circumstances. It creates space to focus on contemplation and the gathering of wisdom. It is the beginning of the moon cycles. It is a time for plotting your course and planning for the future. It does let you unearth new possibilities when you tap into the wisdom of what is flying under the radar. You can embrace positivity, change, and adaptability. If you hope to progress towards your vision, harness the New Moon's power to set the stage for developing your trailblazing ideas. It is a Moon phase for hatching plans for nurturing ideas. Creativity is quickening; thoughts are flexible and innovative. Epiphanies are prevalent during this time of manifestation.

🌒 Waxing Crescent Moon

It is the Moon's first step forward on her journey towards fullness. Change is in the air, it can feel challenging to see the path ahead, yet something is tempting you forward. New information is ready to be revealed; there is a sense of excitement and inspiration in the air. It harnesses a sense of adventure, a willingness to be open to change, and growing your world. This Moon often brings surprises, good news, seed money, and secret information. This Moon brings opportunities that are a catalyst for change. It entices and tempts you to debut your wild ideas and smash your goals. It catapults you towards growth and often brings a breakthrough that sweeps in and demands your attention. Changes in the air, inspiration weaves the threads of manifestation around your awareness.

◐ First Quarter Moon

The First Quarter Moon is when exactly half of the Moon is shining. The other half is in shadow. The Moon will appear as half. It signifies that action is ready to be taken. You face a crossroads; decisive action is going to help clear the path. You can cut through indecisiveness and make a clear path forward. There is a sense of something growing during this phase. Your creativity nourishes the seeds you planted; it does see things are moving forward. As you reflect on this journey, you draw equilibrium and balance the First Quarter Moon's energy before tipping the scales in your favor. You feel a sense of accomplishment of having made progress on your journey, yet, there is still a long way to go. Pause, take time to contemplate the path ahead, and begin to nurture your sense of perseverance and grit as things have a ways to go.

◐ Waxing Gibbous Moon

Your plans are growing; the devil is in the detail; a meticulous approach lets you achieve the highest result. You may find a boost arrives during this time. It gives a shot of can-do energy that helps you progress forward. It connects you with new information about the path ahead. The Moon is growing, as is your creativity, inspiration, and focus. It is also a time of essential adjustments, streamlining, evaluating goals, and plotting your course towards the final destination. Success is within reach; a final push will get you through. It is a time of added inspiration, the wind beneath your wings. The conclusion is within reach, and you have the tools at your disposal to achieve your vision.

🌕 Full Moon

The Full Moon is when you often reach a successful conclusion. It does bring a bounty that adds to your harvest. You gather a sense of recognition and accomplishment. Something unexpected often unfolds that transforms your experience. It catches you by surprise, a breath of fresh air; it is a magical time that lets you appreciate what your work has achieved. It is time for communication and sharing thoughts and ideas. It often brings a revelation eliminating new information. The path clears, and you release doubt, anxiety, and tension. It is a therapeutic and healing time that lets you release old energy positively and supportively. The Full Moon is when people honor her beauty and reconnect with the Full Moon's power.

🌖 Waning Gibbous (Disseminating) Moon

The Waning gibbous Moon is perfect for release; it allows you to cut away from areas that hold back your true potential. You may feel drained as you have worked hard, journeyed long, and are now creating space to return and complete the cycle. Look at areas of your life that didn't reach fruition all that did reach completion, but now you are ready to let that aspect go. It does see tools arrive to support and nourish your spirit. Creating space to channel your energy effectively and cutting away from outworn areas creates an environment that lets your ideas and efforts bloom. It is a healing time, a time of acceptance that things move forward towards completing a cycle. This the casting off the outworn, the debris that accumulates over the lunar month is a vital cleansing that clears space and resolves complex emotions that may cling to your energy if not addressed.

Third (Last/Reconciling) Quarter Moon

This Moon is about stabilizing your foundations. There is uncertainty, shifting sands; as change surrounds your life, take time to be mindful of drawing balance into your world. It is the perfect time to reconnect with simple past times and hobbies. Securing and tethering your energy does build a stable foundation from which to grow your world. It is time to take stock and balance areas of your life. Consolidating your power, nurturing your inner child lets you embrace a chapter where you can focus on the areas that bring you joy. It is not time to advance or acquire new goals. It's a restful phase that speaks of simple pastimes that nurture your spirit.

Waning Crescent (Balsamic) Moon

The Waning Crescent Moon completes the cycle; it is the Moon that finishes the set. It lets you tie up loose ends, finish the finer details, and essentially creates space for new inspiration to flow into your world once the cycle begins again. The word balsamic speaks of healing and attending to areas that feel raw or sensitive. It is a mystical phase that reconnects you to the cycle of life. As the Moon dies away, you can move away from areas that feel best left behind. A focus on healing, meditation, self-care, and nurturing one's spirit is essential during this Moon phase.

Time set to Coordinated Universal Time Zone (UT±0)

Meteor Showers are on the date that they are going to peak.

Spirit Animal Totems

When you harness the power of your spirit animal, you take on their gifts, talents, and abilities. This helps you navigate your life adeptly, and it offers you the power of resilience, tenacity, and perseverance. Here is an alphabetical list of Spirit Animal Totems that may be called upon in this year's Diary:

Alley Cat is active, versatile, restless. Intellectually curious, mentally sharp, and physically agile. Alley cat thinks on its feet and acts with lightning speed to achieve its objective.

Antelope is dramatic and adventurous. Antelope possesses a sensitive and caring nature; a true optimist, Antelope, is convinced that everything will turn out for the best. Antelope is restless and always on the move.

Bernese Mountain Dog is caring and empathetic. They have a somewhat dreamy and detached quality that brings a calm temperament that draws balance. This one has a love of security and home life.

The beetle is a fascinating blend of creativity and spirituality. This totem has an external shell of a warrior, but within their heart resides a poet. The beetle is a gallant crusader for revealing the truth, justice, and equality.

Black Panther has a compelling and persuasive personality. This power animal is complicated, a deep thinker; they resonate with an air of mystery and detachment. A keen observer, they watch and wait for discerning on a course of action.

Bloodhound sniffs out opportunities that are often hidden below the surface. The bloodhound is personable, articulate, determined, and resolute. They have a broad range of interests and passions. Highly intelligent, they use intuitive sensors to access new information. Bloodhound is charming, creative, and remarkably loyal.

Buffalo is a no-nonsense character who believes in rock-solid results. They work hard to achieve a stable foundation. They do best in areas of collaboration and teamwork. Secure, dependable, and practical, Buffalo builds a grounded and stable environment through their passion for results.

Cassowary is a private animal totem who is naturally peace-loving, graceful, and tactful; they avoid conflict and discord whenever possible. The Cassowary is civilized, refined, and aloof. They are self-restrained and contemplative. They consider the consequences before embarking on a course of action.

Chameleon is adaptable and the master of disguise. Outwardly they appear self-sufficient, but they are actually craving companionship and approval. The chameleon seeks positive reinforcement and loves to make a good impression. They possess a strong need for security and companionship.

Chimpanzee is affable, easy-going, and accessible. The chimpanzee has a lively sense of humor and the flexibility of nature that attracts friends and admirers.

Crab is a thoughtful and contemplative truth seeker. This animal totem looks beneath the surface and uses alternative methods to unearth a given situation's truth. Crab quickly tunes into the heart of the matter. This one is secretive, willing to dig a little deeper to discover the underlying reason or validity of any given situation.

Dromedary Camel is practical and hard-working. Ambitious, insightful, and responsible. This animal totem doesn't shy away from challenges; they are fuelled by the prospect of achieving their goals. They are modest, loyal, and generous. This salt of the earth character does what needs to be done and dedicate their attention to the job at hand to achieve a robust result.

Flamingo is charismatic, a natural showman. Flamingo has a vivid imagination and exceptional artistic abilities. Call on flamingo when you need creative help to bring your next project to life. Flamingo thinks outside the box and always does things with flair.

Goose is intelligent, graceful, and elegant. They are in an idealist and believe in the greater good that a positive attitude can achieve. They embrace a close relationship and thrive in a committed relationship. They bond deeply with their partner. They love to travel and seek adventure and won't be restricted or fenced in.

Grizzly Bear is a reserved and gentle being with a deep love of nature. Logical, methodical, and practical, they see the glass as half full and often overlook others' flaws. They are cautious, willing to wait and see the correct path to take before making a firm decision. Their enthusiasm and warm-hearted nature draw others into their sphere.

Kangaroo delivers a message of hope. Kangaroo is modest, charming, and devoted. Being in an outdoor setting and in the wilderness excites and calms kangaroo. Kangaroo is steadfast and loyal.

Killer Whale is a sea creature with a vast creative imagination. Self-assured, the killer whale is a natural leader who resonates with idealism: Channel, the killer whale spirit animal for use in developing innovative projects or for public speaking.

Koi is vibrant, colorful, and dynamic. The life of the party, this animal spirit, loves to circulate and give you confidence when you may feel out of your comfort zone. Getting to know new people is their forte. Inherently idealistic and sympathetic to others' feelings and thoughts, Koi cares about people and their problems. Possessing compassion and magnetism, they soon attract many friends and acquaintances.

Labrador Retriever is charming, gracious, and loyal. Labrador retriever has outstanding social skills and gifts of diplomacy. They desire to be part of the team and have a great deal of pride and ambition to fuel their inspiration. They adore people and companionship and make an excellent contribution to social events.

Leopard is dynamic and born to shine. They possess a creative and courageous spirit that thrives on adventure and excitement. Leopard is not afraid to enter the forest alone, brave and rebellious, wild, and free. Their Knack for flair and innovation sets a bold statement that shocks people out of their complacency.

Lion is fiery and independent. A natural leader and innovative thinker, Lion dislikes taking orders and would instead forge their own path. A born fighter who is easily roused to temper, Lion fights oppression, injustice, and exploitation.

Lobster has a sweet nature, an eternal optimist, lobster sees the good in others. They are highly respectful, attentive, and easy-going. Lobster has exquisite taste and seeks out luxurious environments; this animal totem admires culture, design, and art. Lobster gravitates towards others of a similar refined outlook. This classy animal totem is called upon to encourage upward mobility.

Mosquito is dynamic, versatile, and active. The mosquito animal totem is always on the lookout for new challenges. They are social climbers and have a fascination with watching people. Mosquito is witty, talkative, and entertaining.

Orangutan is a colorful and dramatic character. They think big and set lofty goals. The orangutan has a passion for pleasing others and takes great joy in fulfilling the needs of others. Being of service, relating well to people makes this totem a social and active animal. Orangutan needs plenty of freedom and people who support them to fully thrive.

Owl is an ingenious and visionary guide who is a deep thinker and a robust communicator. Owl spends many hours analyzing the meaning of life before passing on wisdom.

Panda is an intensely private and emotional totem. They have a memory that captures a snapshot of the past, and they find it difficult to let go of old wounds. They are innately curious and love to investigate hidden aspects of people's personalities. They love to be adored, but a tendency towards being an introvert means they prefer this affection at a distance.

Parrot knows a thing about gossip and secrets. They are consummate promoters of ideas, drama, and information. Adventurous and multitalented, the parrot is creative and inspired. Bright flashes of intuition and insight give them a cutting edge that sets them above the rest.

Peacock love to surround themselves with drama and excitement. They are sociable and have an innate desire for companionship: natural confidence and personal magnetism combine with a splashy personality to draw attention. The Peacock loves an audience and thrives on being noticed.

Pheasant is courteous, hospitable, and down to earth. Pheasant has a deep love of home and family life. Their upbeat and sunny disposition wins over friends and colleagues.

Platypus rarely skims the surface; instead, this totem animal digs and probes to get to the root of any given situation. Their easy-going manner attracts friends and companions. Platypus has incredible agility and can multitask among several different undertakings. Their ability to maintain simultaneous projects are a powerful gift they use to create stability. They are usually in perpetual motion, always on the lookout for the right opportunity to translate well into tangible results.

Pomeranian is lively and playful. Always on the go, this animal spirit is intelligent, quick, and vibrant. There is a touch of flamboyance and rebelliousness about them. Pomeranian is openhearted, friendly, and generous. Possessing an upbeat and sunny disposition, their loving and affectionate nature quickly wins you over.

Praying Mantis is disciplined with a youthful air, lighthearted, logical, and agile. Praying Mantis offers a rhythm and dexterity that is exceptional. With acute powers of observation, they choose their words carefully to achieve the desired effect.

Rabbit is quick, restless, and helpful. Rabbit is capable and works hard to build security. This power animal has a frugal nature and teaches us to manage limited resources well and place a high value on home and family.

Raven is an enigma and animal totem with an air of mystery as they can be secretive and suspicious of strangers. Raven is fascinated by life and people. They possess a keen intelligence and can quickly make astute judgments. Call on Raven when you seek to reveal hidden information on situations and people.

Reindeer loves to visit you during the Christmas season. Reindeer is sentimental, family orientated, and sympathetic. With a sunny disposition and warm nature, they are surrounded by close friends. Reindeer is charming, magnetic, and fun-loving. This animal totem loves to party and entertain with friends and loved ones. Warm and generous by nature, they open their home and hearth to social occasions. They are a gracious host, always courteous, diplomatic, and sincere.

Rescue Dog is down to earth, kind, and loyal. They are generous to a fault and may neglect their own needs. They are inclined to carry more than their share on their shoulders. They are drawn to the countryside and the great outdoors. Rescue dog loves the scents and sounds of nature. They intuitively assess people, and their judgment is usually spot on with their character assessment.

Seagull is friendly and reliable. Frugal and able to spot a bargain. They are useful, flexible, and amiable. Seagull is the master of reinvention who doesn't follow conventional rules. Instead, they set their own limits and find challenges that allow them to push gifts and talents further. Evolution and growth are at the crux of their desire to soar higher each day.

Seal is inherently sociable in a friendly manner. They possess an offbeat charm and a playful sense of humor. The Seal totem animal is optimistic and entertaining with a strong sense of self. They are engaging and enjoy social groups. Possessing a magnetic personality, they have a way with people and really appreciate cooperation and teamwork. Friends and family are of utmost importance to this animal guide.

Seahorse is dramatic with a thirst for adventure. Life needs to be stimulating and exciting to keep this animal totem feeling motivated and thriving. They seek relationships that are as deep and passionate as the ocean; their lifestyle is vibrant and soulful.

Snail is honest and optimistic, with a positive approach to life problems. Snail embraces everyday domestic chores; they work slowly and methodically to build stable foundations. They are gifted at projects that involve collaboration and teamwork. Whatever hurdles they face, they usually come up with an innovative workaround.

Spirit Bear has a commanding presence, a big personality brimming with duty and purpose. This animal totem is witty, loyal, and endearing. They are devoted to their work and relationships. An objective thinker, they are deep thinkers who contemplate situations fully before making a decision.

Striped Hyena is an original character who has leadership qualities and an air of authority. They are attracted to a bohemian lifestyle and value freedom over home and security. They are unconventional, radical, and innovative. A wry sense of humor and mischievous nature are their trademarks.

Swan is very sensitive; they are up to date with new trends and resonate grace and style. They thrive on companionship and embrace been in a bonded relationship. They are sensitive and need a harmonious home life. Swan is focused, dedicated, and loyal. An asset to have on your side.

Tomcat is on the prowl and tends to be on the move all night long. They are gifted multitaskers and good communicators. They are drawn to social events and enjoy mingling at night. A sharp mind processes information quickly and tends to dart from one opportunity to the next.

Vulture is independent, assertive, and visionary. This animal totems mind is filled with inspired and cutting-edge ideas. They are quick, decisive, and one of life's warriors. Their exuberant lust for life is magnetic, and they rarely fail to draw magic into their life. Vulture resonates with a powerful influence that repels negativity and fear.

Wolf is a soulful creature who is bright, understanding, and sympathetic. They are a visionary animal spirit with intuitive capabilities that allow them to foresee and anticipate future possibilities. Wolf is independent and adventurous. They crave freedom and excitement. Wolf is an inherent idealist who is a crusader against injustice. Even though they have a tendency towards an unconventional lifestyle, they value companionship and form strong personal bonds.

Zebra like to do things with style. This bohemian character adds a splash of flair to any social occasion. Zebra has a sunny personality and tons of initiative. A true individualist, this animal totem thrives on challenges and new projects. Zebra is essentially a strategist and uses their creativity and resourcefulness to plot the path ahead.

December

Mon 28

Tues 29

Wed 30

Thurs 31

January

Fri 1
New Year's Day

Sat 2

Sun 3
Quadrantids Meteor Shower. Jan 1 - 5, peaks tonight.

Message
Chimpanzee says that you hit upon a new trend that brings positive options to your life. It inspires your mind making you brim with excitement and happiness. Your social life is soon in full swing. You kick off a vibrant phase of developing an area that captures your heart. At the same time, your creativity is heightened, new ideas reach a peak, it does bring a breakthrough moment as you gather insight into the path ahead. It is a time of communication and messages. The news arrives that lets you plot a course towards improving your life. Open communication creates stable foundations, leading to a long phase of enhancing the opportunities for your growth.

January

Mon 4

Tues 5

Wed 6
Last Quarter Moon in Libra at 09.37 UTC.

Thurs 7

January

Fri 8

Sat 9

Sun 10

Message
Alley Cat says that while you are ready to pounce onto a fresh possibility, an aspect of the past influences your current situation; it touches your expectations and aspirations. It does highlight a broad array of options are flowing into your life to tempt you forward. It could have you expanding your horizons and setting off to find a new opportunity. A sense of rejuvenation and renewal suggests that change is surrounding your life on many levels. It has you diverge from your current trajectory and exploring new options.

January

Mon 11

Tues 12

Wed 13
New Moon in Capricorn at 05:02 UTC.

Thurs 14

January

Fri 15

Sat 16

Sun 17

Message

Kangaroo says that this is the perfect time to set up a foundation for the future. Working on the home environment create structures that draw stability into your life. Small actions can have a profound effect. There is a window of opportunity opening that lets you share your insights and ideas with someone who contributes a refreshing perspective to the discussion. It could have you working closely with another on a confidential path that inspires your soul. It is a time of devotion and affection that expands your vision. You create a stable basis from which to grow your world.

January

Mon 18
Martin Luther King Day

Tues 19

Wed 20
First Quarter Moon in Aries at 21.02 UTC.

Thurs 21

January

Fri 22

Sat 23

Sun 24
Mercury at Greatest Eastern Elongation at 02.00 UTC.

Message
Bernese Mountain Dog says that your emotional awareness is finely tuned to the past. The past has a stronghold over your spirit; you miss the good old days. It does bring a sense of longing; your thoughts shape your future goals. The desire for a change of scenery grows ever more reliable. It does have you exploring your options and looking to shake up the potential in your life. A strong emphasis on change brings a path that is a saving grace. You double up on inspiration and plot a course towards developing a passion project. It gets a lift that fuels your emotional tank.

January

Mon 25

Tues 26

Weds 27

Thurs 28
Full Moon in Leo at 19:16 UTC.
Full Wolf Moon.

January

Fri 29
Jupiter in Conjunction with the Sun at 01:00 UTC.

Sat 30
Mercury Retrograde begins in Aquarius.

Sun 31

Message
Owl says that while adjusting to change is difficult, life improves by degrees. A new door opens, and this creates a window of opportunity. It opens the chance to develop your talents. It brings a path that offers room to grow your abilities, and making the most of this direction does see you taking steps to make your dreams happen. It brings active momentum that places a strong emphasis on productivity. Contemplating your creative ideas brings a potent brew of manifestation, pour the essence of your dreams into the cauldron of hope, and see what a recipe for success is written in the stars.

February

Mon 1

Tues 2
Groundhog Day
Imbolc

Weds 3

Thurs 4
Last Quarter Moon in Scorpio at 17.37 UTC.

February

Fri 5

Sat 6

Sun 7

Message

Leopard says that you touch down on some enticing new options soon; this has you reaching for your dreams. You push back boundaries and step out of your comfort zone. Having a fixed goal in your mind sees you taking the steps necessary to climb the ladder of success. A sunny aspect arrives to light a path forward. It is a time which makes you smile; as you push back limitations, you expand your life and focus on the adventure of developing your dreams. This sees you stoking the fires of inspiration. As you move forward, you channel your enthusiasm and see the magic possible when you focus your energy on achieving your goals.

February

Mon 8
Mercury at Inferior Conjunction at 14:00 UTC.

Tues 9

Weds 10

Thurs 11
New Moon in Aquarius at 19:06 UTC.

February

Fri 12
Chinese New Year (Ox)

Sat 13

Sun 14
Valentine's Day

Message
Peacock says that this is the time which rules going after an area that inspires your heart. It is associated with forming a strong alliance with someone who brings joy into your life. Furthermore, the more you think about your romantic goals, the higher your ability to fast track your dreams by utilizing manifestation energy. It does help release limitations and enable things to move forward. Everything that has gone before has been a learning ground; it has provided you with the wisdom, the growth, and the insight necessary to spot the potential possible. You might not have appreciated this person entirely had you not experienced everything else previously.

February

Mon 15
Presidents' Day

Tues 16
Shrove Tuesday (Mardi Gras)

Weds 17
Ash Wednesday ~ Lent Begins

Thurs 18

February

Fri 19
First Quarter Moon in Taurus at 18.47 UTC.

Sat 20

Sun 21
Mercury Retrograde ends in Aquarius.

Message
Orangutan says that with the ending of Mercury retrograde, the atmosphere lightens. You make room for new friends and companions. There is a focus on home and family; opportunities continue to flow into your life teach you to grow and expand your skills. Offering your gifts to others lets you spread your wings. Life takes on a lighter tone; exchanges with friends brings an active and social environment. You build the memories that are moments to treasure. It brings a vibrant time, which is colorful and expansive. It does set the tone for an engaging chapter of fun, friendship, and spontaneity. A surprise ahead brings a boost to your world.

February

Mon 22

Tues 23

Weds 24

Thurs 25

February

Fri 26
Purim (Begins at sundown)

Sat 27
Full Moon in Virgo at 08:17 UTC.
Purim (Ends at sundown)
Full Snow Moon.

Sun 28

Message
Labrador retriever says that your idealism brings warmth into your world; it blesses your life with sunshine. There is an option to give back soon, helping others, being of service brings opportunities that enrich your life. Your life has undergone many changes; reinventing your situation is the perfect way to get new energy into play. It does allow you to remove elements that no longer serve your purpose and stay focused on improving your situation by being flexible and adaptable to change. This is a time that draws abundance into your world, making the most of this chapter does see something of importance arrive.

March

Mon 1

Tues 2

Weds 3

Thurs 4

March

Fri 5

Sat 6
Mercury Greatest Elongation of 27.3 degrees from the Sun.
Last Quarter Moon in Sagittarius at 01.30 UTC.

Sun 7

Message
Lion says that switching into manifestation mode allows you to create growth and activate your creative side; it does draw an option that lights a path towards abundance. Setting your sights on a lofty target, you see your vision growing. Your attention to detail, and your willingness to shift your focus on achieving your goals, show that you are ready to rise to the challenges ahead. It does see you drawing accolades; there is praise for work was done. This feedback motivates you to continue to set the bar high and go after your dreams. There is something in the pipeline, quite substantial, that grows your talents and expands your potential.

March

Mon 8

Tue 9

Wed 10

Thurs 11
Neptune in conjunction with the Sun at 00:00 UTC

March

Fri 12

Sat 13
New Moon in Pisces occurs at 10:21 UTC.

Sun 14

Message
Beetle says that the past has given you a new approach. It is taught you valuable lessons. You discover an entirely different way of dealing with issues. With the hindsight gained, you begin to see the blessings in any challenges that crop up. It gives you a newfound appreciation for your ability to deal with life. Your wisdom is on the increase; stay tuned for a new avenue that grows your gifts further. Things come together over time; it is difficult to become emotionally invested in the outcome, and trying to unscramble mixed messages, can overcomplicate your life. Try to go with the flow and let a bounty of potential unfold naturally over time.

March

Mon 15

Tues 16

Wed 17
St Patrick's Day

Thurs 18

March

Fri 19

Sat 20
Ostara/Spring Equinox takes place at 09:37 UTC.

Sun 21
First Quarter Moon in Gemini occurs at 14.40 UTC.

Message
Panda says that it is a time for contemplation, introspection, and repose. An inner journey this week marks the beginning of a theme of self-development. Signs and serendipity are likely to make themselves known to you; it's all helping you access the right area, which draws healing and abundance into your world. You diverge from your usual routine and head off the beaten track, enabling you to discover a creative journey. It may lead to a new trajectory; it is a path that draws sustenance and abundance, allowing your sense of wellness to heighten. It creates a bold new beginning and sparks positive change. Laying the groundwork carefully provides secure foundations.

March

Mon 22

Tues 23

Weds 24

Thurs 25

March

Fri 26
Venus at Superior Conjunction occurs at 06:00 UTC.

Sat 27
Passover (begins at sunset)

Sun 28
Full Moon in Libra occurs at 18:48 UTC.
Full Worm Moon
Palm Sunday.

Message
Labrador Retriever says that this is an excellent time to organize, prioritize, and streamline. Sifting and sorting through the areas demanding your time and energy enables you to release sites that cause the most considerable disruption. It helps you resolve conflict, and it gives you a definite direction to head down. Fortune favors the bold this week; it brings options to light: creative and social; this draws a sense of connection into your world. If you have been feeling restless, this is guiding you to create space to nurture your life. It brings meaningful activities into your world. It is a boost that has you feeling more enthusiastic about the prospects possible.

March/April

Mon 29

Tues 30

Weds 31

Thurs 1
All Fools/April Fool's Day
Lent Ends

April

Fri 2
Good Friday

Sat 3
Passover (Ends at sunset)

Sun 4
Last Quarter Moon in Capricorn. This occurs at 10.02 UTC.
Easter Sunday

Message
Praying Mantis says that you enter a phase that draws new options to light. It enables you to plot a course towards developing an area of interest. You have talents that require your focus to fully reveal your innate abilities. These gifts will come in handy; they offer you a significant step up to a new level of growth. It opens a gateway, which grows your potential. Focusing on your goals enables you to ascertain a path that is paved with new options. It is a glittering time of discovering opportunities that offer room to grow your life. Taking advantage of these options sees you dazzle with inspiration and enthusiasm as you connect with your personal vision.

April

Mon 5

Tues 6

Weds 7

Thurs 8

April

Fri 9

Sat 10

Sun 11

Message

Wolf says that you have known troubles before, your resilience and tenacity are on the rise. Your patience and perseverance are rewarded, you discover soon, a prominent aspect which brings gifts and luck into your life. Happiness is just around the corner, do your part, stay open to new opportunities, and allow the passage of time to sail you into smoother waters. News arrives, which gives you a boost. Something exciting arrives; this is a high-level option that enables you to progress on your larger goals. Maintaining the focus sees your determination and perseverance come out on top.

April

Mon 12
New Moon in Aries occurs at 2:31 UTC.

Tues 13
Ramadan Begins

Weds 14

Thurs 15

April

Fri 16

Sat 17

Sun 18

Message

Rabbit says that you are transitioning from one life cycle and beginning a new phase. It changes your priorities and has you thinking about the future with a long-term view. As you focus on your dreams, you gain insight into where you are headed. Don't expect everything to become evident at first, as this time offers side paths to explore. A lovely perk arrives soon. This windfall opportunity lets you grow your situation, and you may even decide to branch out into a new area. Life supports your expansion; negotiating the path ahead favors a stable growth phase, which draws heightened security.

April

Mon 19
Mercury at Superior Conjunction occurs at 02:00 UTC

Tues 20
First Quarter Moon in Leo occurs at 06.59 UTC.

Weds 21

Thurs 22
Lyrids Meteor Shower from April 16-25 peaks tonight.
Earth Day

April

Fri 23

Sat 24

Sun 25

Message

Seagull informs that a curious area captures your interest and brings a gift of joy into your life. Acknowledging the signs which guide this journey lets you enjoy an enchanting and magical time. You are entering a time that sees fortune and luck arriving to transition you towards new options. The significant change is the end result of the work you are currently undertaking. It enables you to benefit from a path of substantial advancement. A collaboration ahead brings new opportunities, and you are pleased with the results. Your talents get rewards, taking you towards a new role.

April

Mon 26

Tues 27
Full Moon in Scorpio, Supermoon occurs at 03:31 UTC.
Full Pink Moon.

Weds 28

Thurs 29

April/May

Fri 30
Uranus, in conjunction with the Sun, occurs at 21:00 UTC.
Orthodox Good Friday

Sat 1
Beltane/May Day

Sun 2
Orthodox Easter

Message
Raven shares that you transition towards a significant event that is positive but difficult in the short term. It is a shift that requires strength and fortitude. You soon unearth a quirky yet richly abundant path, heighten opportunities light a new journey forward. This sees you expanding your vision; it enables you to harness wild and rebellious energy and enjoy a chapter of new adventures. A transition is occurring, which is the result of your willingness to be open to new experiences. The pace and rhythm of your life pick up soon; this brings a clear message that things are on the move for you.

May

Mon 3
Last Quarter Moon in Aquarius occurs at 17.50 UTC.

Tues 4

Weds 5

Thurs 6
Eta Aquarids Meteor Shower Apr 19 - May 28, peaks tonight.

May

Fri 7

Sat 8

Sun 9
Mother's Day

Message
Rescue Dog says that your willingness to explore new possibilities opens a unique. It brings a positive aspect that lets your personal life blossom. You take a journey geared towards developing a bond that is dear to your heart. It enables you to enter a social phase that is imbued with the potential to grow your life. It brings a strong focus on developing a journey that is in alignment with your emotional aspect. It does help you strip away areas that are no longer relevant. Refining your goals and aspirations distills the potential possible. It brews manifestation that is potent and inspired. Renewal and rejuvenation are strong themes in the chapter ahead.

May

Mon 10

Tues 11
New Moon in Taurus occurs at 19:00 UTC.
Ramadan Ends

Weds 12

Thurs 13

May

Fri 14

Sat 15

Sun 16
Shavuot (Begins at sunset)

Message
Grizzly Bear says that you have an opportunity to resolve outworn energy and find a solution that creates space for something new and unusual to arrive. This is necessary to achieve your higher goals. There are power and strength in making decisions during this time. A sign comes, which rings especially true; this is helpful and provides insight. Putting yourself first is essential in making that big life change a priority. This resonates through your life as a sense of achievement and abundance flows into your actions and surrounds you with growth potential.

May

Mon 17
Mercury reaches the greatest eastern elongation of 22 degrees from the Sun.
Shavuot (Ends at sunset)

Tues 18

Weds 19
First Quarter Moon in Virgo occurs at 19.13 UTC.

Thurs 20

May

Fri 21

Sat 22

Sun 23

Message

Chameleon shares that a group activity puts you in contact with someone who sparks your curiosity. As you consider the potential with this person, you align with your core dreams and desires. This one is a free-spirited explorer who tempts you to move towards a vista, which is expansive and exciting. It helps you open a path in an area that holds the promise of a happier chapter. Communication soon follows, which helps provide you with objective feedback. This kicks off a high energy cycle that suits your current vision.

May

Mon 24
Victoria Day (Canada)

Tues 25

Weds 26
Full Moon in Sagittarius, Supermoon occurs at 11:14 UTC.
Total Lunar Eclipse in Sagittarius occurs at 11:19 UTC.
Full Flower Moon.

Thurs 27

May

Fri 28

Sat 29
Mercury Retrograde begins in Gemini.

Sun 30

Message
Goose shares that you are ready to set sail on a voyage that draws happiness into your world. There are going to be additional opportunities for you, which open a gateway towards achieving your dreams. Something in the pipeline entices you to begin a new journey. As you start to see an exciting avenue open, you engage in expanding your horizons. There is a willingness to try various options; this gives you the right mix, you will know which path suits you. There are many blessings set to arrive in your life. You resonate with a beautiful aura that draws new potential into your environment.

May/June

Mon 31
Memorial Day

Tues 1

Weds 2
Last Quarter Moon in Pisces occurs at 07.24 UTC.

Thurs 3

June

Fri 4

Sat 5

Sun 6

Message

Black Panther says that if you find yourself feeling sensitive, there is likely still unresolved baggage holding your progress back. Taking time to make peace with what has gone before does draw fresh air into your surroundings. This creates a shift of forwarding momentum, which propels you towards a new chapter of potential. As you heal the past, it makes a more substantial change of potential in your life. You begin to focus on what is truly meaningful in your life; you are less reactive and more heartfelt and spontaneous. It takes you beyond the issues of a previous situation. It enables you to truly become open to the potential which seeks to arrive in your world.

June

Mon 7

Tues 8

Weds 9

Thurs 10
New Moon in Gemini occurs at 10:53 UTC.
Annual Solar Eclipse occurs at 10.42 UTC.

June

Fri 11
Mercury at Inferior Conjunction occurs at 01:00 UTC.

Sat 12

Sun 13

Message
Killer Whale says that having clear aspirations does support the energy coming into your life. As you see things coming together so well, you can pause and reflect on the blessings in your situation. It does signify incredible potential arriving soon. A surprise is arriving soon, which excites your mind. It does change your trajectory, and this is supported by a phase of growth. A shift that transforms you towards an area of higher potential leads to a positive outcome. It does bring you more clarity into a situation you have been concerned about, and it paves the way for an excellent fresh start to emerge.

June

Mon 14
Flag Day

Tues 15

Weds 16

Thurs 17

June

Fri 18
First Quarter Moon in Libra occurs at 03.54 UTC.

Sat 19

Sun 20
Father's Day

Message
Labrador Retriever shares that you incorporate new activities into your world. There are expanded options to engage in social gatherings. It is a pivotal time where you feel your energy shift towards a lighter and more abundant chapter. It does plant the seeds for growth in your social sector; you may even discover a new friendship may blossom under the light of this lively time. This is an ideal time to be bold and propel your progress forward. It has the effect of expanding your life and may even lead to a leap of faith towards chasing a vital dream. As you forge ahead, you draw new potential into your life, which inspires your mind.

June

Mon 21
Midsummer/Litha Solstice. 03:32 UTC.

Tues 22
Mercury Retrograde ends in Gemini.

Weds 23

Thurs 24
Full Moon in Capricorn, Supermoon occurs at 18:40 UTC. Full Strawberry Moon.

June

Fri 25

Sat 26

Sun 27

Message

Seagull says that your spirit is adventurous. Being in touch with your rebellious tendencies, revamps your environment, and creates space for an exciting chapter. An opportunity arrives soon. By keeping your eyes open, you are sure to spot an area ripe for progression. This helps to transform your potential and leads to a soul-stirring time of discovery and adventure. You are ready for an energizing time, enabling you to harness the element of creativity to fire up a golden chapter of inspiring outcomes in your life. You are correct to persevere on your quest towards happiness. Finding that balance between your heart and mind does enable you to draw clarity into your world.

June/July

Mon 28

Tues 29

Weds 30

Thurs 1
Last Quarter Moon in Aries occurs at 21.11 UTC.
Canada Day

July

Fri 2

Sat 3

Sun 4
Mercury at Greatest Western Elongation occurs at 20.00 UTC.
Independence Day

Message
Platypus says innate talents place you in a leadership role where you can teach others. You draw like-minded people into your world; this helps you expand your circle and provides inspiration, which takes you to a different area to develop. You are likely to head to a new site. Several creative opportunities surface, which gives you motivation. As you sort through them, you find the perfect venture to develop. This is a busy time which has you pick and choose among some areas, allowing you to be discerning. A breakthrough occurs, which encourages you to make a firm decision regarding your life path.

July

Mon 5
Independence Day (observed)

Tues 6

Weds 7

Thurs 8

July

Fri 9

Sat 10
New Moon in Cancer occurs at 01:17 UTC.

Sun 11

Message
Parrot informs that this is a highly auspicious time, which suggests luck is on your side. Improvements in your life are indicated. You are being encouraged to be more proactive and pursue what you seek. Making the most of your dazzling talents, you are likely to attract attractive opportunities that provide you with robust growth. As you move out of your comfort zone, you achieve brilliant results. It has the potential to lead to significant change as an influx of fortuitous energy is at your doorstep. Life becomes more dynamic and fun. Your social circle expands as you actively seek and connect with others.

July

Mon 12

Tues 13

Weds 14

Thurs 15

July

Fri 16

Sat 17
First Quarter Moon in Libra occurs at 10.11 UTC.

Sun 18

Message
Vulture says that you enter a dynamic phase that removes deep-seated blocks. It helps you push back the boundaries which have curtailed your progress recently. Any speed bumps or obstacles soon fade away; you leave them in the dust of your inspiration. Your thirst for adventure sees you investing your energy in an exciting area that offers you room to grow your goals. This rejuvenates your spirit. Making a firm decision ahead, you begin to pick up speed. Improvement in your circumstances is a trend that soon gains traction. It is an energizing time, which is exciting and adventurous.

July

Mon 19

Tues 20

Weds 21

Thurs 22

July

Fri 23

Sat 24
The Full Moon in Aquarius occurs at 02:37 UTC.
Full Buck Moon.

Sun 25

Message
Snail says that it's essential to create space to build secure foundations and plot a strategy and vision path. Take the time to build the road ahead carefully and with diligence and perseverance. This offers you the best chance to really make your mark on improving your situation. You begin to see clearly what is possible, which becomes a dramatic tool for you to create the changes you are seeking. It does lead to a chapter of change and growth. Snail sees positive indications that there are some sweet opportunities set to arrive that support your chosen journey. All things come to those who prepare.

July

Mon 26

Tues 27

Weds 28

Delta Aquarids Meteor Shower. Jul 12 – Aug 23, peaks tonight.

Thurs 29

July/August

Fri 30

Sat 31
Last Quarter Moon in Taurus occurs at 13.16 UTC.

Sun 1
Mercury at Superior Conjunction occurs at 14:00 UTC.
Lammas/Lughnasadh

Message
Spirit Bear says that this is a time that motivates a fresh start; it lets you grow your gifts in a new area. Making a commitment to stoke your inspiration's fires gives you a leg up to a new pathway. An offer arrives, which sparks an active phase of growth; the conditions are right to achieve a stellar outcome. Change is in the air; a fresh wind of potential arrives to bring stability and security gifts. It helps you build secure plans; remarkably, it's not as difficult as you may currently be believing. Someone is willing to help, and this person can offer their wisdom and life experience. This gives you a helping hand towards a chapter that allows you to grow your ambitions.

August

Mon 2
Saturn at Opposition occurs at 05:00 UTC.

Tue 3

Wed 4

Thurs 5

August

Fri 6

Sat 7

Sun 8
New Moon in Leo occurs at 13:50 UTC.

Message
Seal says that you tie up some loose ends, reflecting and integrating the chapter, which has recently occurred. As you pause and reflect on the past, you activate a sense of renewal. It creates space to release outmoded areas and resolve any feelings which are holding you back. This creates a beautiful environment for drawing something new into your life. Opportunities soon come knocking to tempt you forward. You discover a mentor who opens doors; this is someone you can lean on for guidance; this helps you clarify your ideas and bring relevant information to light. Taking stock of where you currently enable you to chart a course towards an active growth phase.

August

Mon 9
Islamic New Year

Tues 10

Weds 11

Thurs 12
Perseids Meteor Shower Jul 17 - Aug 24, peaks tonight.

August

Fri 13

Sat 14

Sun 15
First Quarter Moon in Scorpio occurs at 15.20 UTC.

Message
Pomeranian says that an offer crops up, which feels like a good fit. It sparks a productive chapter, which gets you thinking outside of the box. Expanding your horizons does broaden the options available. It takes you to a time of building stable foundations and gently moving forward. This is a time that sees you moving forward. It is a productive time that lights up an aspect of self-expression. It takes you towards developing a closer connection with someone meaningful. This leads to an adventurous chapter, and it does hit the sweet spot, providing you with plenty of inspiration.

August

Mon 16

Tues 17

Weds 18

Thurs 19
Jupiter at Opposition occurs at 23:00 UTC.

August

Fri 20

Sat 21

Sun 22
Full Moon in Aquarius, Blue Moon occurs at 12:02 UTC.
Full Sturgeon Moon.

Message
Zebra shares that this is a time that kicks off a rejuvenation chapter. It brings new foundations, and it does see you improving your living situation. A smart and insightful person helps open the door for you to progress a larger goal. Things are on the move for your life; it does see a transit occurring where you release the doubts. When you de-clutter your life of anxious thoughts, you begin to focus on developing a path aligned with your vision. This takes you towards a highly organized chapter, and it is a boon for your stability. There are a lot of options coming up, which draw good fortune into your world. It gives you ample inspiration to explore.

August

Mon 23

Tues 24

Weds 25

Thurs 26

August

Fri 27

Sat 28

Sun 29

Message

Lion shares that you establish a position of authority and, restrictions which have been an issue recently are lifted. It may prompt you to look at your business plans, see where you can pull in areas, and jumpstart other areas that heightened productivity. You begin to see those rock-solid foundations emerging, which gives you a sense that things are progressing nicely. You have many gifts to share with the world, and your creative offerings will take you places. A time of transformation does take you towards building your dreams in the chapter ahead.

August/September

Mon 30
Last Quarter Moon in Gemini occurs at 07.13 UTC.

Tues 31

Weds 1

Thurs 2

September

Fri 3

Sat 4

Sun 5

Message

Crab says that you may have felt under pressure recently, and if it feels that the demands on your time are crowding your creative freedom, there is a sunny sky arriving soon. It brings news which offers you room to focus on an area that rejuvenates and restores equilibrium. This gives you the freedom to chart a course that draws happiness and joy. It sends curiosity and inspiration into your life. Maintaining a flexible approach will help you adjust to the changes ahead. It is an extraordinary time to focus on self-development. This sets off a brilliant chain of events that draws abundance into your life.

September

Mon 6
Labor Day

Tues 7
New Moon in Virgo occurs at 00:52 UTC.
Rosh Hashanah (begins at sunset)

Weds 8
Rosh Hashanah (Ends at sunset)

Thurs 9

September

Fri 10

Sat 11

Sun 12

Message

Flamingo says that in terms of manifestation, your creative abilities are sharp and at a heightened level. It provides you with the skills which help you make the most of this exciting chapter. An offer crosses your path, which takes you by surprise; it does allow you to spread your wings and expand your abilities in a new area. It is the perfect way to compliment your current life; you create space to level up your situation, bringing you to a happy outcome. Your willingness to explore new areas plays a part in this successful chapter. You enter a phase that offers you room to progress your goals. It is an especially crucial phase that creates harnesses the power of adventure to good effect.

September

Mon 13
First Quarter Moon in Sagittarius occurs at 20.39 UTC.

Tues 14
Mercury at Greatest Eastern Elongation occurs at 04:00 UTC.
Neptune at Opposition occurs at 08:00 UTC.

Weds 15
Yom Kippur (begins at sunset)

Thurs 16
Yom Kippur (Ends at sunset)

September

Fri 17

Sat 18

Sun 19

Message

Dromedary Camel says that you will have the right opportunities to improve your circumstances soon. It is exciting, as you have been under a cloud, which limited your progress. The options which arrive focus on self-development and improving your home environment. It beautifully orients you towards a chapter that is a wellspring of abundance; it also suggests support coming to grow an idea of yours. You benefit from more stability, which becomes a core foundation that will sustain you in the chapter head. If you have found yourself feeling restless, this is a key to expanding your options.

September

Mon 20
Full Moon in Pisces occurs at 23:55 UTC.
Full Corn Moon. Harvest Moon.

Tues 21
International Day of Peace
Sukkot (Begins at sunset)

Weds 22
Mabon/Fall Equinox. 19:21 UTC

Thurs 23

September

Fri 24

Sat 25

Sun 26

Message

Buffalo says that a great deal of happiness and positivity is set to emerge in your life. It tempts you towards an enticing chapter, which offers you a wellspring of options to explore. A remarkable achievement is ahead. This does place a spotlight on growth. It gives you much appreciated recognition for the work you have undertaken recently. It does bring life events that are memorable and offers you a chance to expand your horizons. Under a social sky, you discover room to spread your wings and enjoy sharing thoughts and ideas with others.

September

Mon 27
Mercury Retrograde begins in Libra.
Sukkot (Ends at sunset)

Tues 28

Weds 29
Last Quarter Moon in Cancer occurs at 01.57 UTC.

Thurs 30

October

Fri 1

Sat 2

Sun 3

Message

Mosquito says that an invitation to attend an event that captures your interest. Mingling with other kindred spirits, you feel a connection with those who hold similar interests. It does hit a sweet spot. Remarkably, the timing is right to connect with someone of importance. It does suggest that your social life is about to become very vibrant and joyful. It sees you making swift decisions, following your intuition, and developing a closer bond with this dynamic character. It initiates a wave of transformations surrounding your life; you negotiate a path which balances your goals with a blended approach with this person.

October

Mon 4

Tues 5

Weds 6
New Moon in Libra occurs at 11:05 UTC.

Thurs 7
Draconids Meteor Shower. Oct 6-10, peaks tonight.

October

Fri 8
Mars in Conjunction with the Sun occurs at 04:00 UTC.

Sat 9
Mercury at Inferior Conjunction occurs at 16:00 UTC.

Sun 10

Message
Lobster says that a generous offer makes itself known to you; this provides you with an option that enables you to focus on your goals. It has you feeling optimistic about your prospects; you enter a phase of robust growth and productivity. This makes a big difference to your bottom line. It does show you have more control over the path ahead. You hold the reins and manifest an active phase of growth. It leads to a lucrative chapter, as this is a path that blesses you on many levels. Options are coming, which provides you with new ideas, and this continually evolves your potential and grows your gifts. It does see your talents being shared with a broader audience.

October

Mon 11
Thanksgiving Day (Canada)
Indigenous People's Day
Columbus Day

Tues 12

Weds 13
First Quarter Moon in Capricorn occurs at 03.25 UTC.

Thurs 14

October

Fri 15

Sat 16

Sun 17

Message

Seahorse informs that a new flow of inspiration generates an exciting chapter. It gives you a burst of motivation to accomplish a long thought goal. It is a time where you have more to look forward to, as it also brings the news out of the blue to inspire a phase of growth. It is time for you to shine as opportunities arrive to support a stable period of transition. It is a busy time that harnesses a creative aspect to develop a venture that captures your interest. Your curious mind is ready to dive deep and explore a path that offers room to progress your goals. It is an extraordinary time of sharing thoughts and ideas and creating a fantastic brew of potential.

October

Mon 18
Mercury Retrograde ends in Libra.

Tues 19

Weds 20
Full Moon in Aries occurs at 14:57 UTC.
Full Hunters Moon.

Thurs 21
Orionids Meteor Shower. Oct 2 - Nov 7, peaks tonight.

October

Fri 22

Sat 23

Sun 24

Message

Panda says that you may have been through a difficult time, and Panda wants you to know that you have the strength to adjust the course as necessary. The path ahead offers you a chance to renew and rebuild. Your spirit thrives in an environment that is creative, spontaneous, and active. There is plenty to keep you motivated and excited about life; it brings changes that give you the freedom to focus on an expressive phase. New energy is coming; it opens a refreshing flow of potential opens enticing paths of opportunity; this gives you plenty to feel inspired about. Concentrating on developing your dreams will set you on a mission that brings joy into your life.

October

Mon 25
Mercury Greatest Western Elongation occurs at 05:00 UTC.

Tues 26

Weds 27

Thurs 28
Last Quarter Moon in Leo occurs at 20.05 UTC.

October

Fri 29
Venus Greatest Eastern Elongation occurs at 22.00 UTC.

Sat 30

Sun 31
Samhain/Halloween
All Hallows Eve

Message
Pheasant says that this is a significant time where you can focus on improving your home environment. It draws new energy into your life. If you have found things have been stale recently, this is set to lift with a refreshing flow of potential, which shakes up the options in your world. It corresponds with a path that draws abundance. There is activity coming, which shines a light on a productive chapter. It creates the basis from which you propel your dreams. It denotes new friendships arriving, leading to fun events on the horizon. It stimulates your mind and encourages a more expansive landscape.

November

Mon 1
All Saints' Day

Tues 2

Weds 3

Thurs 4
New Moon in Scorpio occurs at 21:15 UTC.

November

Fri 5
Uranus at Opposition occurs at 00:00 UTC.

Sat 6

Sun 7

Message
Parrot is excited to share that you shall be presented with a unique opportunity; this supports a growth phase and begins a new chapter. It is an area close to your heart, which is a welcome boost to your spirit. It sees you dotting the lines on an exciting phase of self-development. An opportunity crosses your path with a flourish; it brings a sea of potential that gives you a valid option to grow. This area harnesses the power of your creativity. As ideas and inspiration are peaking, it charts a course, which offers you exceptional potential. It does see new options unfolding soon.

November

Mon 8

Tues 9

Weds 10

Thurs 11
First Quarter Moon in Aquarius occurs at 12.46 UTC.
Remembrance Day (Canada)
Veterans Day

November

Fri 12
Taurids Meteor Shower. Sept 7 - Dec 10, peaks tonight.

Sat 13

Sun 14

Message
Owl says that you discover an insightful path that's in alignment with your higher calling. It sees you embark on a karmic journey. You may experience a sense of déjà vu; it draws a unique environment where you can use your own magic brand. Exploring this potential sees you expanding your horizons; you exhibit courage and daring. It sets the stage for an adventure that draws many blessings. Creating a sacred space where you feel safe to nurture your dreams lights a path to your higher self. It brings abundance into your life. You benefit from a fresh flow of energy, which kicks off a new cycle of growth. This is rejuvenating as it encompasses both healing and new growth.

November

Mon 15

Tues 16

Weds 17

Leonids Meteor Shower Nov 6-30, peaks tonight.
Partial Lunar Eclipse.

Thurs 18

November

Fri 19
The Full Moon in Taurus occurs at 08:58 UTC.
Full Beaver Moon.

Sat 20

Sun 21

Message
Koi says that circulating in your wider community does bring a powerful new influence into your life. It sets the stage for an enterprising time which sees you socializing and kicking back with kindred spirits. It harnesses a sense of creativity, as you feel encouraged to share your wisdom with others. A new and vital chapter is coming; it does see you embracing a new flow of activity. This is a time where you shine a light on a powerful influence; it drops a creative element into your lap. You feel drawn to artistic expression and may find yourself absorbed in a new area. It is a time made for fun with friends; social invitations light a shimmering path forward.

November

Mon 22

Tues 23

Weds 24

Thurs 25
Thanksgiving Day (US)

November

Fri 26

Sat 27
Last Quarter Moon in Virgo occurs at 12.28 UTC.

Sun 28
Hanukkah (begins at sunset)

Message
Platypus says that serendipity draws abundance into your life. An offer crosses your table, which contains an excellent advantage. Suddenly, the path ahead clears; it brings out a succession of events which give you some unique new options to consider. Under this powerful influence, you achieve a stable phase of progressing your dreams. The future looks bright, and this has you thinking strategically about future planning. You optimally advance your situation by nourishing your environment and providing the right landscape for growth.

November/December

Mon 29
Mercury at Superior Conjunction occurs at 05:00 UTC.

Tues 30

Weds 1

Thurs 2

December

Fri 3

Sat 4
New Moon in Sagittarius occurs at 07:43 UTC.
Total Solar Eclipse.

Sun 5

Message
Swan feels there is little to hold you back. Given the reins, you can move swiftly forward. You have an eye for detail, and an innovative approach will bring dividends into your world. It is a time which is exciting, expansive, and new adventures await your open heart. News arrives, which offers you a chance to develop your talents in a refreshing environment. There is activity afoot in your social aspect, and this is a breath of fresh air; it gives you a new lease to expand your life. An array of opportunities and pleasant surprises arrive, friends, seek you out, and visits to events are likely.

December

Mon 6
Hanukkah (Ends at sunset)

Tues 7

Weds 8

Thurs 9

December

Fri 10

Sat 11
First Quarter Moon in Pisces occurs at 01.36 UTC.

Sun 12

Message
Reindeer says that this is a time for expanding your social circle. New friendships are coming, giving you a wonderful sense of happiness. Some personal goals are coming to fruition soon. It is an opportune time for contemplating the path ahead. Taking time to focus your energy on developing a social aspect leaves you feeling enthusiastic about the prospects possible. It connects you with a broader world of opportunity; this places you in the box seat to expand your life and deepen the ties which bind.

December

Mon 13

Geminids Meteor Shower. Dec 7-17. Peaks Dec 13-15.

Tues 14

Weds 15

Thurs 16

December

Fri 17

Sat 18

Sun 19

The Full Moon in Gemini occurs at 04:36 UTC.
Full Cold Moon, Full Moon Before Yule.

Message

Kangaroo says that nurturing bonds is a balancing act. The art of this diplomacy smooths over conflict. However, those who stir up drama only drain your precious energy; distancing yourself from people who take advantage of your nature helps set appropriate boundaries. Nurturing your creativity is also essential; new options are arriving to tempt you towards growth and artistic expression. There is good energy coming around home and family, be aware that tension limits potential. If you feel stuck, spend time releasing stress. You soon lift the lid on an exciting chapter of potential. It does light a path that offers abundance and while giving you space to achieve your goals.

December

Mon 20

Tues 21
Ursids Meteor Shower Dec 17 - 25, peaks tonight.
Yule/ Winter Solstice occurs at 15:59 UTC.

Weds 22

Thurs 23

December

Fri 24
Christmas Day (observed)

Sat 25
Christmas Day

Sun 26
Boxing Day (Canada & UK)
Kwanzaa begins

Message
Labrador retriever says that things are coming together for you soon. It brings a time of positive communication and a sense of community into your world. She feels that support is coming from a surprising ally. It does get you a long-overdue shift towards abundance and smooth sailing. There is also creative energy swirling around your vision; taking time to disconnect from distractions will help you tap into new ideas. Broadening your perception that you tap into an abundant landscape ready to be developed following your higher vision.

December

Mon 27
Last Quarter Moon in Libra occurs at 02.24 UTC.

Tues 28

Weds 29

Thurs 30

December/January

Fri 31
New Year's Day (observed)
New Year's Eve

Sat 1
New Year's Day
Kwanzaa ends

Sun 2

Message
Goose says that focusing on expanding your horizons does see you forge ahead towards an exciting chapter. You enter a time that offers good fortune and luck; this could land a windfall in your lap. It leads to dazzling days where you negotiate an exciting chapter that provides a variety of options. It does extend good vibrations around your aura. The energy you resonate with is reflected in your life. Keeping a positive and optimistic outlook sets the scene for an incredible phase of abundance. Set your sights high, and know that you can soar above limitations and achieve your chosen destination.

Notes

Notes

Notes

Notes

Notes

About Crystal Sky

Crystal is passionate about the universe, helping others, and personal development. She writes yearly horoscopes diaries for each star sign. She produces a range of astrologically minded journals to celebrate the universal forces which affect us all. You can visit to learn more about Crystal's books and personal astrology readings by visiting the website.

www.psychic-emails.com

When not writing about the stars, you can find Crystal under them, gazing up at the abundance that surrounds us all, with her pup Henri by her side.

www.ingramcontent.com/pod-product-compliance
Lightning Source LLC
Chambersburg PA
CBHW051807040426
42446CB00007B/556